Movie Trailer Mastery

VOICE OVER AND VOICE ACTING

Movie Trailer Mastery

THOMPSON HOWELL

Voice Over and Voice Acting:

Movie Trailer Mastery

Published by www.complete-voiceover.com

Copyright © 2020 KTPR, Inc.

No part of this publication may be reproduced, stored in a retrieval system, or transmitted in any form or by any means, electronic, mechanical, photocopying, recording or otherwise, without the prior written permission of the publisher. For permission, contact the publisher at publisher at info@complete-voiceover.com.

Disclaimer of Warranty, Limitation of Liability. Neither the publisher nor the author make any representations or warranties with respect to the accuracy or completeness of the contents of this work; and they specifically disclaim all warranties, whether express or implied, including without limitation fitness for a particular purpose. No warranty may be created or extended by sales or promotional materials. Nothing contained in this work is to be considered as the rendering of legal, accounting or other professional advice for specific cases, and readers are responsible for obtaining such advice from their own professional counsel. Neither the publisher nor the author will be liable for any loss, damage or injury arising from or related to this work. The fact that an organization or website may be referenced in this work does not mean that the author or the publisher endorses the information that such organization or website may provide or any recommendations it may make. Further, readers should be aware that Internet websites listed in this work may have changed or vanished between this work's creation and when it is read; and neither the author nor the publisher are responsible for any such websites (or their content). Unless expressly stated, the author has received no compensation for any products and services mentioned herein. All product and company names are trademarks™ or registered® trademarks of their respective holders. Use of them does not imply any affiliation with or endorsement by them.

For free voice acting lessons with videos, visit:

www.Complete-Voiceover.com

ISBN: 978-0-9828863-7-3

Visit **Complete-Voiceover.com** for more books on voice over and voice acting.

Visit **ThompsonHowell.com** for reels and more information.

More books from Complete-Voiceover.com:

The Voice Over Startup Guide:
How to Land Your First Job

ABOUT THE AUTHOR

Thompson Howell received his acting training from the highly regarded theater department at Northwestern University and worked in Chicago as a voice actor and radio personality for many years before making Los Angeles his home in 2006. He works from his broadcast quality home studio located just down the street from the Warner Bros. lot.

A native of Boston, he is an accomplished organist and also ran the 2005 Chicago Marathon in 5 hours, 15 minutes, and 31 seconds.

Some of Thompson's trailer campaigns include *Acrimony* (2018) and *A Simple Favor* (2018), both for Lionsgate, *The House with A Clock In Its Walls* (2018) for Universal, *The Report* (2019) for Amazon Studios, and *Uncut Gems* (2019) for A24.

Twitter: @Thurston3rdVO

Instagram: thurston3rdvo

Facebook: @ThompsonHowell.VO

Web: www.ThompsonHowell.com

Contents

Introduction ix

1 *Where We've Come From* 1

2 *Finding Your Own Trailer Voice* 11

3 *Give The People What They Want* 17

4 *Representation* 47

5 *Opportunity Knocks: Auditioning* 57

6 *You Booked It!* 79

7 *Sustaining A Career* 87

8 *The Future* 95

Introduction

I took my very first voice over (VO) class in 1986, and back then, if you had told me that I'd one day have the chance to narrate movie trailers, I wouldn't have believed you.

Well, I have gotten to voice trailers! The path to achieving that success was definitely challenging and it didn't happen overnight, something that can be said of working in any area of the voice over industry.

But getting into the world of movie trailers is especially tricky. It is small, it is insular, and it is competitive. I worked in voice over for years before understanding how to become a member of the movie trailer talent pool. My path was made more difficult by the lack of resources available. Until now, if you wanted to work in movie trailers and their associated marketing campaigns, there was no guide to follow.

I'm going to change that. I'd like to help you forge your own path to trailer work. There's never been a better time to take the journey if you're willing to put in the effort. A dream coupled with a persistent attitude can pay off. If you've already been pursuing a voice acting career, you know exactly what I'm talking about.

The Voice Over Pyramid

First, though, I think it's important to understand the current state of the voice over industry. There's

Introduction

a clearly defined hierarchy of work in our business. I call it the Voice Over Pyramid. It is very wide at its base and not very tall, and is made up of all the various kinds of work done by voice actors.

At the bottom are the bread and butter jobs such as IVR (interactive voice response), e-learning, corporate narration, and audiobooks. This work is usually available to voice actors through online avenues and can be done without the help of a talent agent. No one complains about doing these jobs, but they're not very lucrative on a per-job basis. One must perform a relatively high volume of them in order to make a living working in just these areas alone.

In the middle of the pyramid you might find commercials, a genre that can be much more lucrative. Many spots provide talent with a long tail of income, with buyouts and residual payments that keep coming long after the session wraps. Once the exclusive domain of talent in larger markets, commercials are now booked by talent globally thanks to the internet. But there's less of this work available, and competition is tougher for these jobs.

As we rise up the Voice Over Pyramid, the space begins to shrink as the number of opportunities to work decreases and the skill level to thrive increases. Above commercials you might find promos (network, cable and affiliate), animation, and video games, all work that requires certain skill sets possessed by fewer voice actors.

And right up there at the very tip of the Pyramid is the world of doing movie trailers. It is generally considered the most elite area of voice acting. It's certainly the most lucrative when you're lucky enough to voice a campaign and, because it's so competitive, it has the fewest number of people working in it.

That means you'll need all the help you can get if you hope to join the ranks of go-to trailer voices. It's challenging, but not impossible, to break through and grab a seat on the bench.

Introduction

My Story

As a kid growing up in 1970's Boston, I was fascinated with microphones at an early age. My parents' old cassette tape recorder, a clunky thing we kept in the hall closet, was one of my favorite toys. I would often take it out and record myself doing bad celebrity impressions. In elementary school I was intrigued with the public address system. During special events I'd hang out by the announcer's table hoping they'd let me say something really important into the microphone. To hear my own voice come out of those speakers was a thrill.

After graduating from the theater program at Northwestern University, I put my interest in microphones to good use as a radio disc-jockey. It's something I'd always dreamed about after growing up on a steady diet of Top 40 radio stations filled with larger-than-life personalities. Working at a real radio station brought my love of music together with my desire to perform.

I had taken my first VO class just months before starting my first radio gig because I'd heard about this thing called freelance voice acting. What a great way to use my acting training, I thought! Being at the radio station only fueled my interest even further.

The rest, as they say, is history.

The entire voiceover business has changed so much since I got into it around 30 years ago. It's become a lot more competitive as more and more people have thrown their hats into the ring. But the good news is there are things you can do–things you have control of–that can help your chances of being successful as a voice actor even in an area such as movie trailers.

Working at the top of the Pyramid requires certain skills, and I'm going to show you some ways to develop those skills and hone your trailer narrating chops. I'll show you how to find your trailer

Introduction

voice and explain the kind of help you'll need. My goal is to help you stand out as a viable creative option for the people who can hire you.

Pursuing work as a narrator for movie trailers takes dedication and patience. To be a player, you need to understand the game you're playing.

Reading this book is a great start. My aim is to share as much information as possible. My years of experience are all here. I'll share the ups and downs and show you how to meet the challenges and share in the breakthroughs. And I'll try do it in an entertaining way. I want you to have fun as you learn!

No two voice acting careers are identical, so you shouldn't expect your path to look exactly like mine. But we can both end up at the same place. I'm excited to share the practical tips, stories, and career advice that moved the needle of my own career.

As the saying goes, every journey begins with a single step. Let's begin.

Get The Audio

We've put together a collection of audio files to go along with examples in this book. They're available to download for free at www.complete-voiceover.com. The link is at the top of the home page. Reading about voice over is great, but your learning will be much more complete if you also hear examples of voice over work.

We recommend first saving the files to your computer. From there you can add them to your media library and transfer them to your tablet, phone or any other device. They are mp3 files, so you can import them into a sound editor, or even burn them to a CD. If you need technical support, please email us via the site's contact form.

Kindle/eReaders

To get the most out of this book, turn off column viewing and hold your Kindle in landscape mode.

Get your audio now for free. You'll learn so much more if you do!

WWW.COMPLETE-VOICEOVER.COM

CHAPTER 1

Where We've Come From

"You're gonna need a bigger boat."

(JAWS, 1975)

So, what exactly is a movie trailer anyway? And why is it even called a "trailer?"

Beginning in 1913 when the first trailer is known to have been produced, movie theater owners would show short films promoting soon-to-be-released movies. Today we call those coming attractions. Thing is, these shorts were shown *after* each feature presentation. Reels of film were delivered to theaters "tails out," meaning the end of the film was easily accessible on the outer edge of the reel. Rather than rewind the film to the beginning, theater owners would simply edit a trailer onto the end of the film because it was easier. It *trailed* the main feature and earned the nickname, "trailer."

But theater owners quickly realized that most people would simply leave after watching the movie they came to see. That problem was solved by screening trailers to a captive audience *before* the feature presentation, a practice that continues to this day.

Technically, short films promoting an upcoming feature aren't really trailers anymore, but the name stuck and today we use the term to describe not only the traditional trailer shown in movie theaters, but also the entire gamut of audio/visual marketing for a film that may run on TV, radio, online, and on mobile devices.

While the overall purpose of a movie trailer has remained constant over the decades, their production value has evolved, a result of advancements in technology along with shifts in attitudes and expectations in society at large. Movie marketers have always tried to make their trailers stand out in clever and unique ways. A trailer is essentially a commercial for a film and, like in all areas of advertising, a client wants their product to be on the top of every consumer's mind.

Thanks to the internet, it's really easy to trace the stylistic evolution of trailers because so many of them are available to view online. We'll get to the audio files you downloaded from www.completevoiceover.com in a bit, but for now, head to YouTube if you want to view the trailers referenced below.

The Evolution of Trailer Narration

The trailer for 1939's "Gone With the Wind" uses a voice over that is very presentational, almost like a newsreel or old time radio announcer.

https://youtu.be/0X94oZgJis4

His elocution is perfect; his tone is stentorian. He's the voice of authority telling you about the film and why you should see it.

Now watch the trailer for "Jaws" from 1975, released by Universal.

https://youtu.be/4pxkU9GVAoA

It opens with a sequence from the point of view of someone, or some *thing*, traveling underwater. Then begins the narration by a deep voiced man speaking in a calm, deliberate tone as he slowly describes the "creature" and how it has survived millions of years of evolutionary changes; how it is a ruthless "eating machine;" how it only desires to attack and devour anything in its path. Then there's a quick cut to a female swimmer gently treading water in the calm, moonlit ocean just as the shark takes its first bite from below.

"Jaws" was really the very first true summer blockbuster. Testing a new two-part marketing plan, Universal heavily promoted the film far in advance of its release including a huge merchandising effort. Then it paid for a massive prime-time TV campaign over several days just before the film opened. The strategy worked. The studio built up incredible anticipation about the yet-to-be-seen shark. The trailer's hyperbolic copy, together with the dramatic delivery of the narrator, helped to make "Jaws" the highest grossing film to date at the time.

Now look at 1988's "Die Hard" starring Bruce Willis.

https://youtu.be/jaJuwKCmJbY

"It's Christmas Eve in LA, and New York cop John McClane has come to see his wife…" Instead of objectively telling us *about* the story as the narrator in the "Gone with The Wind" trailer did, this narrator is actually telling us the story itself as it unfolds with a tone that's intended to invite us into the world of the movie and draw us in to what's happening on the screen. This is generally the approach used in trailers to this day.

Now jump to one of the longer trailers created for "Titanic," the 1998 Academy Award wining film for Best Picture directed by James Cameron.

https://youtu.be/ezcvpLIyifU

Yep, no voiceover at all for the entire 4 minute and 9 second duration! But in another trailer, we hear the soft, dulcet tones of Don Morrow sharing an invitation for us to "Take a journey back in time…"

https://youtu.be/jUm88F3MEbQ

His voice is emotional, gravelly, gentle. It's as if he's breathing the words into the microphone. The focus is not on the disaster of hitting the iceberg and how the ship sank. It's on the personal story between Rose and Jack that the film portrays.

"Titanic" was sold as a love story–that unfolded during one of the most storied tragedies of the 20th century. The announcer on the "Gone with The Wind" trailer from 58 years earlier seems like he's almost shouting at us by comparison.

We can look to the trailer for Guillermo del Toro's 2018 Academy Award winning film "The Shape of Water" as a fine example of using the voice of a character in the film to provide the narration which begins, in this case, with only a single sentence.

https://youtu.be/XFYWazblaUA

The trailer opens with the camera moving slowly through a room that's completely under water. Furniture floats around in an elegant dance as soft light from above illuminates the scene. Then the voice of actor Richard Jenkins, who plays Giles in the film, quietly speaks. "If I told you about her... what would I say?"

It's an effective use of a character's narration to quickly pull us into the world of the film, and a gentle reminder that not all impactful trailers need to use an external narrator at all. And that makes the path to trailer narration success that much more challenging.

There are plenty of other trailers we could look at, but the evolution of trailer narration is clear: the reads have become more intimate and the narrator is almost part of the story being told on screen.

Story Matters

What any trailer voice talent keeps in mind is this: a trailer needs to tell a compelling story no matter it's length, even if the only scripted words are the title of the film and its rating.

A trailer's main goal is to elicit an emotional response from viewers. Trailer producers want to give audiences an idea of the experience they're going to have when they see the movie. Will they laugh? Will they cry? Will it be the "thrill ride of the summer?" Perhaps audiences will be more scared than they've ever been! A well-made trailer sucks you into the world of the film and invites you to experience something you'd never get at home.

The key to being a really good narrator in a trailer

or any of the related audio/visual elements in a campaign is to be a good story teller. You need to develop the emotional capacity to revel in the horror films, chuckle at the comedies, to feel the importance of the epic dramas, and to laugh and cry simultaneously at the romances. And do all of that using the words you're given to speak.

Good storytelling takes acting skills and an understanding of some of the techniques that make listening to a well-told story enjoyable. In Chapter 3, we'll take a look at some trailer copy, and I'll show you how to bring those scripted words to life. First, though, I want to talk briefly about finding *your* trailer voice.

CHAPTER 2

Finding Your Own Trailer Voice

"Words mean more than what is set down on paper. It takes the human voice to infuse them with deeper meaning."

—MAYA ANGELOU

Your Voice Print

If a friend walks up behind you and speaks, how do you know it's them? By the sound of their voice, right? Just like finger prints, no two voices are exactly alike. There may be similarities but they're not identical. It is the unique characteristics of each of our vocal mechanisms (lungs, larynx, vocal chords, etc.) that make our voices sound the way they do.

As human beings, we each have our strengths and weaknesses. By virtue of any number of factors, some of us are just better equipped to do certain things than others. The same is true of our voices. In the world of voice over, certain voice prints are better suited to certain types of copy than others. This is as true in the trailer arena as it is with commercials. Our life experiences help inform our point of view, our sense of humor, our sense of wonder, our doubts, our fears–everything. Our voices really can say a lot about us and a great voice actor brings all of that life experience to the stories he tells. When the authentic "you" shows up in your reads, that's when the magic happens.

So how do you find your own unique voice?

Imitation Leads To Learning

We've all heard that imitation is the sincerest form of flattery. We tend to imitate what we're drawn to and like as a way of trying to understand it experientially from our own point of view rather than as an observer. Young babies do this a lot. They learn language by trying to imitate our sounds and over time they learn to talk. They respond with a giggle to our facial expression as we playfully stick out our tongue at them. They might make a funny face back at us to see how we respond. As they get older they may use their imagination to pretend they're Superman or they may want to be just like their favorite baseball player, or a policeman, or a fireman, and so on. It's playing.

We can do this as adults too. When I first started as a radio disc-jockey, I tried to sound like one of my radio heroes at the time who was working at a competing station. I admired the on-air persona he developed and tried to imitate his sound. Of course, I never sounded exactly like him at all, but it was my way of learning to be better at what I was doing from someone who I thought was the best at doing it.

As you begin the journey of learning to be good at voicing movie trailers you'll probably find yourself imitating a lot of what you hear, and I'm here to tell you: that's okay–in the beginning. Imitation is a great way to begin to understand why that particular voice print works (or doesn't) with that copy; why the narrator's interpretation of the copy works (or doesn't); what if feels like to do the job.

Learning Leads To Authenticity

As you progress, your understanding of what makes a good trailer read will increase, more and more light bulbs will go off in your head, and you'll finally "get it." Your confidence in what you're doing will increase substantially and your reads will become more authentic as a result. You'll be able to analyze copy more quickly, and your reads won't just be imitations anymore. You'll be taking ownership of them. More of your individual, authentic voice will show up in them, and that will make you a better storyteller.

I could get ten equally qualified and well suited voice actors to read the same trailer copy. All of the talent will probably deliver terrific, bookable reads in line with what the studio is looking to use on the campaign, but I will guarantee you this: they will all be different. It won't be about who read the copy best. It becomes a decision about which read best matches with the story the studio wants to tell. It's a selection, not a competition, and it's these kinds of decisions that trailer production houses and studios make each time they cast a trailer narrator.

There are other non-creative considerations too–but we'll touch on those later.

So–let's move on to why you really bought this book! In the next Chapter, we'll take a look at some trailer copy, and I'll show you how to make the words on the page come alive.

CHAPTER 3

Give The People What They Want

"You just put your lips together and blow."

(TO HAVE AND HAVE NOT, 1944)

As we've learned, movie trailers have evolved over time and continue to do so. Today, flashy graphics and attention-grabbing footage from the film dominate trailers. Some don't use a narrator at all and those that do might just have the narrator say the movie's title and rating at the end. There also might be a release date at the start or finish. No matter the amount of copy, the role of the narrator is to help tell the story the trailer or TV spot is trying to convey.

Did your parents read you bedtime stories? Did you ever sit around a campfire on a warm summer night and tell ghost stories with your friends? When it came to your favorites, even if you knew everything that happened and how they ended, you enjoyed hearing them over and over.

Why? Because your parents and campfire pals were always fully invested in the act of telling the story! They didn't read it in a flat, disinterested voice. No, they took the time to make the story compelling to hold your interest as a listener. They'd create excitement, or anticipation, or a sense of wonderment with their tone of voice. They varied their pacing and got a kick out of your reaction to their delivery, even if they didn't think of it in those terms.

Narrating a film trailer or TV spot uses essentially the same skills. Sure, you have fewer words to speak than that ghost story which makes you jump, but your investment in the telling of the tale is paramount.

As a narrator, your goal is to give people a glimpse into the experience they're going to have when they see the movie. Don't worry about what they're going to *think*. What's important is how they're going to *feel*.

Folks who go to see a comedy want to laugh. If they're watching a sappy romantic comedy, they want to cry when things all work out in the end. When they flocked to theaters to see "Jaws" back in 1975, they knew full well they'd be really scared. They *wanted* to see the shark terrorize the small beach town of Amity Island.

So, give the people what they want!

The Process

Before I start talking about ways to bring trailers to life, I want to clarify something. I'm assuming you've been pursuing voiceover in another area and that you're used to analyzing copy. If you've looked at and worked on a decent amount of commercial, promo, and narration copy, then you already have a head start in dealing with trailers.

Some aspects of trailer copy analysis might also apply to other VO genres, but because the trailer read is so highly stylized, there may be some things you'll learn here that won't work well in other areas, particularly commercials. Today's reads for TV commercials trend heavily toward a very real, non-announcery sound, but a trailer read is hardly that! Nobody goes out in public and speaks with a trailer style voice unless they intend on getting a lot of strange looks.

If anything feels over your head, I recommend

brushing up on commercial copy analysis with another book in the *Voice Over and Voice Acting* series, "Commercial VO Strategies: Tell a Story, Land the Job" by Chris Agos. Or, if you're new to the voice over business, get started the right way by reading "The Voice Over Startup Guide: How to Land Your First VO Job."

Elements of A Trailer Read

Every piece of copy is different, but there are some general techniques that can be applied to most any copy to make it fun to hear and bring the story of the film alive. Like all written copy in any area of voice acting, the words on the page are not meant to be read, they're meant to be said.

Like the conductor of a symphony orchestra, a trailer narrator can use a combination of elements to bring out the "music" in the copy in order to best convey the story it tells. Pitch, phrasing, silence, pacing, dramatic pauses and other such components of good storytelling are tools you can use to help build your performance.

With that in mind, I'm going to give you some tools to orchestrate your reads. If you haven't already, now would be a good time to visit www.complete-voiceover.com and download the audio files associated with the following examples.

Volume

Great storytelling draws people in, and in a movie trailer you don't have to speak very loudly. In fact, the more quietly you say the words, the more listeners will lean in to hear.

Imagine yourself in a theater watching a trailer. The theater lights go down. There's the film footage, the graphics, the music, and then the narrator begins. Even if he's speaking in a whisper, the voice is being amplified over the theater's elaborate sound system. These days, you may even be watching a trailer on your phone or tablet. Those smaller screens on our personal devices create an even closer, one-on-one relationship with the viewer. There's no need for a lot of volume, even if it's a trailer for a wacky comedy.

The goal should be to bring a sense of intimacy to your reads. Listen to the difference between these examples.

Examples 3a–3c:

"The Shape of Water. Rated R."

The Pause

When someone is speaking to you and they pause in the middle of a sentence, what's your natural reaction? You want to hear what they're going to say next to complete their thought, right?

For example, if I walk up to you and say, "Hi, my name is…" followed by silence I'm pretty certain you'd wait for a second before giving me an inquisitive look because you want to know my name and expect I'm going to tell it to you. Finally, I say, "... Thompson Howell" to complete my sentence and give you the information.

The copy for the *Jaws* trailer I referenced in Chapter 1 is much longer than what's normally written today, but it illustrates a good point about the effect of pauses. If you give it one more listen, you'll hear the narrator using plenty of them. Let's apply that technique to a different script, and since we're in the thriller genre, we'll stay there.

> *In the forests of our world, there are ancient beings. They are like us, yet nothing like us. Bypassed by evolution, they follow no laws, possess no morals, apply no logic. For millennia, they have watched and waited. Until now.*

The film is called "Sasquatch", and tells the story of a group of super strong humanoid giants who, after millennia of avoiding humans, have come out of hiding to violently claim their place in the world.

Writers of trailer copy are always thinking about the editing process and how the words will fit into the final version of the produced trailer. If this script were to show up in your inbox as an audition, it would probably be written out like this:

Example 3d:

"In the forests of our world...

There are ancient beings.

They are like us yet nothing like us.

Bypassed by evolution...

They follow no laws...

Possess no morals...

Apply no logic.

For millennia...

They have watched and waited...

Until now.

Sasquatch: Nowhere to Hide

Rated R"

Read it out loud in your normal speaking voice. This allows you get the main idea of the copy and discover any words or turns of phrase which might cause you to stumble.

Then, read the above copy in an attitude that takes on the overall tone of the movie. I think the copy itself gives you a pretty good idea of what the tone of the film is, but you can always use the online resources that are available today to do more research about the film.

What's the experience the audience will have when seeing the movie? Do you notice how dramatic tension increases by breaking the copy into different sized phrases while pausing in between them? Each successive phrase builds on the one just before it. The audience is watching the trailer and listening to the story with anticipation as it unfolds bit by bit. Some of the pauses might be longer, some could be shorter; that's really the job of the voice actor to figure out, but a dramatic pause of any length helps create the suspense that a trailer like this one is designed to create. Experiment! Think like an editor and give them options to work with.

Now let's add even more interest to the read by looking at the line "They follow no laws." Read it out loud, but add a slight hesitation between the words "follow" and "no." How does that feel? What effect does it have?

Examples 3e & 3f:

"They follow no laws."

"They follow...no laws."

I think it gives the narrator a great opportunity to do something interesting with the words "no laws." It's as if the narrator speaks the words "They follow..." and then has a moment to consider just the right words to come after, and he chooses the words "no laws." It also helps play up the unexpected contradiction to the usual relationship between the words "follow" and "laws."

There are other opportunities for pauses. Where? Take a look at the line "They are like us yet nothing like us." At this point in the trailer, all we know is that there are ancient beings in our forests. Add a big pause in between "us" and "yet." What affect does that have? By splitting the line up in this way, the narrator has a great opportunity to really work the second half of the line in a menacing way that sets up the copy that follows it and clearly defines the dark tone of the film.

Examples 3g & 3h:

"The are like us yet nothing like us."

"They are like us...yet nothing like us."

Paying attention to details like this can really

make a read stand out. It shows that an actor is on the writer's side.

Call it a pause, a break, a lift, or a hesitation... always watch for the opportunities to make the copy more captivating by adding tension and suspense.

Leaning

Leaning into a word is a way of giving it a little extra emphasis. This technique gives certain words a bit more importance than the others. It's subtle. It isn't like fully accentuating a word with extra volume. It's more like an elongation of a word by playing around with the vowels. A coach I've worked with calls this, "letting the word bloom."

Want a simple, classic example?

In a world...

This phrase was coined by the late, great Don LaFontaine, who is said to have voiced around five thousand trailers during his long career. He was the quintessential movie trailer guy with a voice that could cut through a busy action/adventure trailer with lots of visuals, graphics, and dramatic sound design. If you needed a voice that could cut steel, Don was your guy.

Although the "In a world" setup isn't used much anymore, it helps to illustrate the effect of leaning into a word.

In this case that word is "world." Regardless of whatever copy comes after it, that word needs to be important. You can't rush through it! Try giving it just a little more importance by leaning into it, gently elongating the middle "er" sound without increasing your volume. Simply saying the word louder would hit it too hard and break the momentum of the line you're speaking.

Example 3i:

"In a world..."

Now try saying the line in your regular speaking voice without paying any attention to the word "world."

Example 3j:

"In a world..."

Now say the line in your "trailer voice" with the intention of capturing the imagination of those who are watching the story you're telling.

Example 3k:

"In a world..."

You could almost substitute the line above with "Imagine a world..." which is precisely what you're trying to convince the audience to do. By giving "world" that little more expansive, elongated reading, you're drawing the audience in. It's a tiny bit of vocal magic that invites everyone to suspend their disbelief and enter into the world of the film they're going to see. Again, a trailer's job is to give people a sense of the experience they'll have when they go along for the ride and see the movie.

Let's take a look at another example. Sometimes the film's subject matter can give you clues about which words you might lean into. Is there a word in the copy below that stands out to you as being a candidate for leaning?

A lawyer...

branded as an outlaw.

An outlaw...

revered as a leader.

A leader...

hailed as a legend.

Madiba: Slow March to Freedom

Rated PG-13

I vote for "legend." Why? Well, the subject of this film is a man who served 27 years in prison for his stance against apartheid in his country and would later become the nation's first black President under a democratic constitution. But there's another reason that the word "legend" deserves some special treatment.

The Rule of Three

The Rule of Three says that when you're presented with a list of three things, or three phrases in a row of similar construction, you always give the third item a different treatment than the first two.

In the copy above we have Phrase 1: "A lawyer branded as an outlaw." Phrase 2 is: "An outlaw revered as a leader." And Phrase 3 is: "A leader hailed as a legend." Let's say you want to round out the cycle of 3 phrases with a downward inflection of the word "legend" while also leaning into it gently for soft emphasis. In that case you need to treat the first two phrases in a slightly different way.

The goal is certainly to connect the phrases and

create a through line for the read that logically connects them all together. We need to hear the progression from "lawyer" to "outlaw" to "leader" right on through to "legend."

With that in mind, have a listen to Example 31 to hear what I mean.

Example 31:

"A lawyer...

branded as an outlaw.

An outlaw...

revered as a leader.

A leader...

hailed as a legend.

Madiba: Slow March to Freedom

Rated PG-13"

Here's another similar but slightly different example. It's different because there are actually four similarly constructed phrases. It's hard to know why the writer broke the typical pattern here, but you still have to give each phrase it's due while making that last phrase the one that brings it all home.

There are places...

that define us.

People...

who understand us.

Events...

that make us question our faith.

Moments...

that conjure our darkest emotions.

This is a piece of copy that can easily incorporate all the techniques we've touched on so far: The Pause, Leaning, and The Rule of Three. Practice, practice, practice! We'll revisit this piece of copy a bit later.

The Eyebrow Raise

The Eyebrow Raise is a variation of the leaning technique that uses a certain sing-songy vocal inflection to suggest that the narrator knows something more about the story than the viewer. It draws extra attention to a particular phrase or sentence within the body of the copy intended to elicit from the audience a sense of curiosity, wonder, mystery, and intrigue.

Right now, lift up your eyebrows. What physically happens? Your eyes get wider and your face lifts as your forehead wrinkles. Your jaw probably opens a little wider too. How do these physical changes in your face make you feel? Have you just received some unexpected news? Have you just witnessed a terrible accident? Maybe you've just realized something deep and profound about yourself or someone else you thought you knew well. The Eyebrow Raise intends to mimic that sentiment by using your voice to subtly point out a significant detail in the copy.

Here's some copy for a film about a mysterious castle:

Welcome to a castle...

with memories...

mysteries...

and a mind of its own.

The Clairvoyant Castle

Rated PG

This kind of copy begs for a "storyteller read," one you'd hear from somebody telling you about a magical place in a far away land that you've never been to. What can we tell about the film's story given the copy?

Well, there's a castle. It's apparently clairvoyant, meaning it can see into the future and perceive things beyond normal human sensory perception. How is that even possible for a non-living thing? Wait—it has memories. Not just that, but it says the castle has a mind of its own! That's pretty unusual. I have questions.

What does having "a mind of its own" mean? Does it think? What kind of memories can a castle have? Is the castle nice or is it evil? I'm curious about that.

If you're curious as the narrator, how can we make the audience feel the same? Add a little Eyebrow Raise to the phrase "and a mind of its own" in addition to any other pauses or leaning possibilities throughout the script. That inflection will indicate the specialness of this castle: the fact that it has a mind, that it thinks, that it's actually self-aware.

Example 3m:

"Welcome to a castle...

with memories...

mysteries...

and a mind of its own.

The Clairvoyant Castle

Rated PG"

Here's some copy for a film called "Date Night." It's about a couple in their 30's, Seth & Angie, who plan a regular date night every couple weeks as an antidote to their busy work lives. But when their respective exes show up together at the same restaurant, comedy and a little awkwardness ensues.

What they thought was a normal date night...

Is about to become more than a date.

Date Night.

Rated R.

Thursday.

Which line gets your vote for an Eyebrow Raise? I think it's, "Is about to become more than a date." *How* it's about to become more than a date is what everyone wants to know. Suggest to the audience that they'll have to see the film to find out the answer.

This film is a dark comedy. If it were an intense suspense thriller, you could read the line in a slightly more menacing eyebrow raise tone. If it were a light comedy, you'd use a lighter tone to convey the idea that the wackiness that ensues in the film is all caused by some crazy misunderstanding. In reality, the film's a hybrid so the tone ought to be not too dark and not too light. Right down the middle.

Example 3n:

"What they thought was a normal date night...

Is about to become more than a date.

Date Night.

Rated R.

Thursday."

The more trailer copy you work on, you'll see there are certain writing patterns that show up again and again. While each piece of copy is different, The Pause, Leaning, The Rule of Three, and The Eyebrow Raise are some techniques you can use to bring that copy to life and make you a better storyteller.

Critic Spots

Critic spots are TV commercials which recount the praise lavished on a movie by film critics. You'll probably read more copy in a critic spot than you will in any other kind of trailer.

If a studio feels a movie has a high chance of being well received, they will arrange advance screenings for film critics prior to it's public release. The hope is, of course, that good reviews will drive ticket sales. It's a marketing plan that multiplies viewership, similar to the way viral videos spread from viewer to viewer.

If people see a film based on the positive opinions of critics who like it, those people are likely to tell friends how good it was. Then those friends will go see it and *they'll* tell some friends, and so on. If there are a lot of positive reviews for a movie, particularly if it has the potential to win awards, the studio will order a critic spot or two in which the narrator will recite key words or phrases from some of the critics' actual reviews.

Here's a sample of a critic spot for a hypothetical film that has been nominated for the Academy Award for Best Picture–and has a really good chance of winning:

This January...

The Red Desk is being hailed...

As one of the best films of the decade.

Nominated for four BAFTAs.

And winner of three Golden Globes

Including Best Picture.

It's "glorious."

"Superbly entertaining."

"Audiences will be cheering."

The Red Desk

In theaters January 28th.

Spots like this are typically produced during awards season in advance of the Academy Awards when the film has already been nominated for and perhaps won other prestigious awards. That's usually an indication that it has a good chance to win for Best Picture at the Oscars. Besides the general public, critic spots are intended for one strategic target audience: awards voters!

The key to reading a spot like this is to do it with a feeling of prestige and reverence. It's a respectful sounding read spoken with an even, heartfelt tone, not a hyped up sales pitch. It's as if you're trying to communicate, "This motion picture is so important that you absolutely must not miss seeing it yourself."

Find those words and phrases in the copy that you can gently lean into to give them extra importance. Perhaps "hailed", "best films of the decade", "four BAFTAs", "winner of three Golden Globes", and "Best Picture." When you get to the actual quotes from critics, let them be the star of the show; don't gloss over or rush through them. They are the whole point of producing the spot in the first place.

Example 30:

"This January...

The Red Desk is being hailed...

As one of the best films of the decade.

Nominated for four BAFTAs.

And winner of three Golden Globes

Including Best Picture.

It's "glorious."

"Superbly entertaining."

"Audiences will be cheering."

The Red Desk

In theaters January 28th."

Give The People What They Want

One technique I find helpful in giving each word its due is to make the "air quotes" gesture as I read each quote. If you have another gimmick that works better for you and achieves the same result, use it!

CHAPTER 4

Representation

"Show me the money!"

(JERRY MAGUIRE, 1996)

By now you've realized that the industry doesn't just let you into the top of the Voice Over Pyramid. You need help to get there.

The entertainment marketing business, which includes the production of trailers, is really a people business. Unlike many other genres of voiceover, you won't find auditions for trailers online. Talent agents and managers will be your only source for these opportunities. Let's talk about each for a bit.

Talent Agents

As a general rule, commercial talent agencies with a strong footprint in voiceover have large rosters of talent working in many corners of the VO industry. They may also represent performers for on-camera commercial work and theatrical productions. The individual agents who work at an agency are essentially salespeople. Generally, long established agencies tend to have far better footprints in voiceover than others. There are A-list agencies just as there are A-list actors.

Think of agents as being the people who handle the day-to-day activities relating to your career: searching out and receiving opportunities, coordinating auditions, submitting talent demos as requested, and negotiating the contract when you book a gig. Because you are not their only client, a talent agent can give you and your career only so much of their time.

Voice Over Managers

Voice over managers, however, work exclusively with voice talent and are very selective about the talent they represent. They are the people who have the strongest relationships to talent buyers in the entertainment marketing areas of promo and trailer. They have much smaller rosters than a talent agency and are able to give each one of their talent more of their attention.

Managers help develop, grow, and sustain a talent's career over the long term. They're the "big picture" people. All careers have seasons and when a good manager commits to you, and you to them, they will shepherd your career through its ups and downs, twists and turns.

The reality is that if you're going to actively pursue being a trailer narrator, you're going to eventually want both an agent *and* a manager working for you. Typically, you'll start being repped only by an agent who will help in developing your career to a certain point. If you show promise as a trailer talent, your agent might recommend you to one of the voice over managers who can really help take your career to new levels.

A less usual scenario is that you're discovered first by a manager who is then able to help place you with a talent agent they feel would be best for you. Agents and managers who share talent have learned to work well together for the benefit of all. No matter how your path to representation unfolds, everyone wants things to work smoothly.

Your entire representation team will make money when you do so it's in everyone's best interest to help you to be a talent whose career is always growing. These pros, *especially* managers, have invested years in developing relationships with talent buyers at the trailer production houses and studios, resulting in direct access to audition opportunities for the talent they represent. With the power to hire talent in the hands of so few people, you're going to need this kind of help to share in that access.

But not just any agent or manager will do. The truth is that in order to pursue trailer narration, you'll need an agent in Los Angeles and/or New York even if you don't live in either of those cities. There are a couple reasons for this.

First, experience counts. Agents who book voice actors on movie trailers are going to have much stronger relationships with trailer producers and movie studios than those who don't. Also, all of the voice over managers representing trailer narrators are based in these big coastal cities.

While most of the Voice Over Pyramid has gone global, trailer work is still pretty local. There are few movie studios and even fewer trailer production houses to service them. It's a small world, and trust is important because of what's at stake. The studios spend lots of money to market their movies! If a studio is choosing between two equally qualified and talented narrators to voice a campaign, and will pay one of them a tidy sum for doing so, they usually go with the voice they know and trust who is repped by an agent or manager with whom they've worked before.

So your aim should be to land with one of those agents or managers. Frankly, I cannot think of a single person who has voiced movie trailers who did not have both an influential agent and a well-connected manager to help build their careers.

Unfortunately, you just can't march into an agent's or manager's office and demand that they represent you–even if you're really talented and ambitious. Each agency and manager has submission policies that you can usually discover on their respective websites. Follow them! Some reps welcome general submissions from anyone while others will consider a submission only if it's from an industry referral.

Ultimately, talent representatives get to decide if *they* want to represent *you*; it doesn't work the other way around. If a talent agency's roster already includes a handful of people who share your signature voice print, chances are that agency will take a pass.

Because they have much smaller rosters, managers are even *more* selective than agents. I will say this: if you're fortunate enough to land a proactive agent and an attentive manager you need to treat them as part of your team. And remember–there is no "I" in "team!"

My manager tells a story about something that happened when she had just started her business. A highly successful and well known voice talent at the time was interested in her services and arranged to have lunch with her to discuss the possibilities. She arrived early, sat down at the table and waited patiently. Apparently the talent was running late but hadn't taken the time to let her know. Finally the big shot talent showed up very late, plopped himself down in the chair across from her, looked her in the eye and arrogantly asked, "So? What can you do for me?"

Lunch ended early.

Now, if you don't happen to live in LA or New York, don't worry. With all of today's technology allowing for real-time audio connections between distant locations, such as Source-Connect, ipDTL, and even good ol' ISDN where it's still available, agents and managers can work with talent all over the country–and the world. While anyone can seek out representation using a rep's stated submission guidelines, there are two ways you can put yourself in the best position to get results.

The first way is if a trusted and accomplished voice actor refers you to their agent or manager. If the talent is well respected, a recommendation

Representation

should open a door. Have friends who are already represented in LA or New York? Ask them if they'd consider submitting your demo to their reps. I've done this if I think there might be genuine interest on the part of my agent or manager. It doesn't always pan out, but remember: "No" today doesn't necessarily mean "No" tomorrow.

If you happen to meet an agent or manager at a VO training seminar or workout group, that's the second way to generate interest. At these gatherings, they have a chance to hear your work, which is half the battle in finding representation. If they express interest after meeting you, it's because they think they might be able to fit you into their roster.

If you're wondering about commissions, you'll usually be paying each of your representatives 10% of your gross earnings, assuming you're working a job under the jurisdiction of SAG-AFTRA, the union of professional media performers. Yes, that's 20% of your gross earnings if you have both an agent and a manager, although there are some managers who operate using different compensation agreements with their talent. Some people question the need to have both. My experience has been that my income has increased having both even though I'm paying more out in commission.

The question of whether to join a union is a whole different conversation, but know that in the United States, trailer jobs are typically done under a union contract which stipulates the minimum scale rate you are to be paid. That's "minimum." A good agent or manager is usually able to negotiate for more.

CHAPTER 5

Opportunity Knocks: Auditioning

"It's the editor who orchestrates the rhythm of the images, and that is the rhythm of the dialogue, and of course the rhythm of the music. For me, the editor is like a musician, and often a composer."

—**Martin Scorcese**

So, you've got your new representation team in place. You've become a good interpreter of trailer copy using the techniques I showed you earlier. People are fired up to get your name out there as a new player with a bright future in voicing movie marketing campaigns! Yay!

Now what? Scratching!

Eventually you'll receive the first of many e-mails from your manager or agent with a request from a talent buyer looking for some "scratches" for a movie trailer or TV spot they're working on. Scratching is auditioning, and it's the job you'll probably do the most as a narrator. Unless you're booked on the final edit, you won't get paid for your audition, but it's still important that you do your best because you're going to have an audience–people who could hire you.

Why is it called a scratch? I'll answer that question in a bit, but at this point let's talk about how

Opportunity Knocks: Auditioning

the whole audio/visual part of the film marketing process works.

The Process

As Martin Scorcese alludes to above, it's really a film's editor that orchestrates the rhythm of a film. Great editing can make a mediocre film seem a lot better. Bad editing can make an otherwise brilliant masterpiece miss the mark.

Well, a movie trailer is really a short version of the movie it's promoting and trailer editors work hard to use all the movie's elements to create compelling mini-films that sell tickets. This includes the voice over narration.

A scratch request will usually come from a production house that specializes in creating film trailers and other related audio/visual marketing tools for the studios. Sometimes a studio will contract with several production houses to produce different parts of a campaign. You may get several requests for scratches from more than one source for the same film, and you almost certainly won't be the only talent recording them.

The marketing effort for a film can begin many months before the movie is actually released. First, a teaser trailer might be created which is intended to create excitement about the release of a longer trailer sometime in the future. Teasers might be produced before editing on the film itself has even been completed. This happens a lot with big summer blockbusters. Think about the "Star Wars" films. That franchise's audience can't get enough trailers for each new movie.

After the teaser, they'll release a more substantial trailer for the film, which will include more footage than the teaser trailer did. Much of this material will be distributed online on sites like YouTube or social media platforms. It's all about attracting ears and eyeballs!

Finally, a few weeks before a film's actual release

Opportunity Knocks: Auditioning

date, the TV, radio and digital spots will be planned and created. The process is more intricate and sophisticated than the "Jaws" campaign was back in 1975, but the intention is the same: build audience interest in a film long before it shows up in theaters.

How The Narrator Fits In

Due to the variables involved in developing the audio/visual components of a marketing campaign, flexibility is required in creating and editing all of these pieces together.

Unlike a commercial or TV promo where the voice over is usually the very last element to be added to the final product, a trailer is created almost in the opposite fashion. As part of an editor's process of assembling a trailer and orchestrating its rhythms, a narration scratch track is created to get a feel for what the trailer might look and sound like when it's completed. Unless the read is exceptional, this track will eventually be "scratched" from the finished product and a new voice track will be recorded for the final version.

Production houses will receive a number of scratch tracks from a small handful of voice actors. Then they'll decide which actor's tracks they want to use in their editing process. Once they've finished their work, they will send the finished product to the studio executives for final approval, including approval on the voice.

Sometimes an actor who has provided the winning scratch track will get the nod from the studio and their original recordings will be used in the final cut. But this can't happen unless your files are broadcast quality, which requires using professional-level equipment in your home studio.

If your copy interpretation is great and the technical quality of the recording is really good, it makes it easier for the studio to book you because they don't have to record any new voice tracks. That takes up time and they usually want to get things done sooner rather than later.

There are times, however, when copy changes will necessitate the need to record some new lines or even just a single word. It has nothing to do with you but just understand that the editor wants those changes as soon as possible. In reality, he wanted them the second he was alerted of a change. Don't keep people waiting!

Scratch That!

Now that you understand the purpose of scratch tracks and how they fit into the overall trailer editing process, I'm going to walk you through a mock audition and explain how I'd go about scratching for this particular piece of copy. There is no single right way to do anything; this is the way that works best for me. You need to take the information, guidelines, and techniques I've shown you and come up with a work process that works best for *you*.

Because I already touched on this copy briefly back in Chapter 3, let's work on it some more since we've already got a head start on it. Here's the copy that's just arrived from my manager in my Inbox:

There are places...

that define us.

People...

who understand us.

Events...

that make us question our faith.

Moments...

that conjure our darkest emotions.

Notice how the copy itself doesn't mention the title of the film at all. Check the subject line of the e-mail, and I'll bet you'll find it there. Usually, your manager will forward an e-mail from a production house seeking scratch reads and the project title will be listed somewhere in that message or its subject line.

Once you identify the title of the movie, you can search for more information about it online. I usually use a search term using the film title followed by the word "movie." I could also go directly to IMDb.com (Internet Movie Database) and check for it there. From this quick search, I can discover the director of the film and if any major stars are going to play leading roles. If the film has an established director and/or well known actors attached to it, you know the film is a big deal and will come with some heavy marketing to support it. You can also read a brief summary of the film's story which will give you an idea of its tone. In this case, it's a dark one.

From here, you can search on YouTube to see if there's a trailer posted there. There might be more than one, actually. Even if there's no narrator on them, watching them is going to tell you more about the story, the characters, and the general tone of the movie. Is it a comedy? A romance? Nope. In this case, it's definitely a drama/mystery. All of the information you've gathered so far gives you an indication of the tone your reads will need to have.

As I've mentioned before, time is of the essence. Read that e-mail from your manager again. I'm pretty confident it's going to say that reads are due back "within the hour" or "within 30 minutes" or maybe "ASAP!" You don't have until tomorrow sometime. You need to do your homework, script analysis, recording, editing, and return e-mailing within a pretty short period of time. The more experience you gain, the more quickly you will sharpen your skills and be able to turn scratch requests around in a timely manner.

Now let's look at the copy itself. Back in Chapter 3, I used this script as an example of a variation of the Rule of Three. There are actually four similarly constructed phrases in this script that we need to deal with:

- **Phrase 1:** There are places that define us.
- **Phrase 2:** People who understand us.
- **Phrase 3:** Events that make us question our faith.
- **Phrase 4:** Moments that conjure our darkest emotions.

As we showed earlier, trailer copy isn't written out in complete sentences. A writer will typically break up the phrases on the page, which gives you a clue as to how she hears the pacing of the narrator's delivery in her head. It also opens up some possibilities about the way an editor will combine the narration with the visual images used in the trailer.

Several things are clear to me as I review the copy. First, I see the clear through line of the script using the anchoring words "places," "people," "events," and "moments." As I look at the script on the page, I also see how I can use vocal pauses to break up each phrase into separate parts and use leaning on each of the anchor words to give them a little extra meaning. I can also clearly use the Rule of Three (in this case four) to help each phrase build on the one just before it. Remember, the narrator is not being heard in a vacuum. The voice that's drawing us in by creating dramatic tension is being heard up against the visual elements that the editor chooses to use together with the rest of the sound design, particularly the musical score. Everything works together.

Now I'm going to put on my editing cap so I can think like an editor. It's possible that all the copy will be read as one chunk. That is, without rushing the read, each phrase will follow the one before it without any long breaks. In this case, each phrase must still receive its due.

An editor could also choose to break the read up in a way that allows for some kind of punctuating visual or audio element that occurs in between each phrase. It could be a piece of dialogue from the movie; it could be a closeup on the face of a character who's in the middle of some grand realization; it could be some change in the music; it might be a combination of things. You can't be sure. But you can be the editor's best friend by giving him options. The way you deliver the narration might trigger a brilliant creative editing idea that he might not have thought of otherwise that will put you at the top of the list of contenders for the job.

Given all of the above analysis and my past experience, here's how I'm going to lay down the scratch tracks for this copy:

First, I know that breaking up each of the phrases into shorter "mini-phrases" helps build tension for the viewer. I'm going to read them that way as I read the complete script from top to bottom a couple of times. I'll start with a moderate pace, making each read just a little different from the other:

Example 5a:

(moderate pace)

"There are places...

that define us.

People...

who understand us.

Events...

that make us question our faith.

Moments...

that conjure our darkest emotions."

Now I'll read the entire script again top to bottom two times with a slightly faster pace. This will give the editor not only a faster read of the whole script but will give him quicker reads within each individual line too. He may create a "Frankenstein read" marrying parts of one take with parts of another.

Varying your pace gives him the opportunity to do that if he needs to:

Example 5b:

(quicker pace)

"There are places...

that define us.

People...

who understand us.

Events...

that make us question our faith.

Moments...

that conjure our darkest emotions."

Next, I'm going to record a set of "ABC's" of each phrase in the copy. I'll read each one three times in a row and make each read slightly different from each other without changing the overall tone of the read I've established. This is where you get to change up the pacing and your use of The Pause, Leaning, The Rule of Three, and The Eyebrow Raise. These changes will be subtle and shouldn't be distracting. Let's start with the first three phrases. I've got something special I want to do with the fourth and final phrase later:

Example 5c:

(3 in a row of each phrase)

"There are places...

that define us."

...then...

Example 5d:

"People...

who understand us."

...and then...

Example 5e:

"Events...

that make us question our faith."

Finally, I'm going to read three in a row on the last phrase. As we've learned, that last phrase is really the most important and the one that you need to treat differently than the first three.

You can sense that the drama has been building throughout the read and on the screen too. The editor is sure to choose a really important moment from the film to follow the last line of copy, and I want to set that up as best I can by doing two things. I'm going to add a slight pause between the words "conjure" and "our." Can you hear the effect that will have? It'll set up the answer to "conjure *what*?"

Then on "our darkest emotions," I'm going to do a little Eyebrow Raise because I know something dramatic is about to happen in the trailer, and I want to communicate that to the viewer. I'm also going to do a slight variation of the Eyebrow Raise that'll really infuse extra meaning into the words "darkest emotions." I guess you could call it the Furrowed Brow read. I may read a few extra takes on this phrase just to be sure I've covered my bases and given the editor extra options.

Example 5f:

"Moments...

that conjure...

our darkest emotions."

Now that I've recorded all the reads I intend to send, all I need to do is put a name slate at the beginning of the recording, edit out any long gaps between reads to save space, and save the work as a .wav file.

It never hurts, however, to take a few extra steps to make your audio a bit more presentable and user friendly for the editor. There is no single standard way of doing this. I usually take the time to edit out all the breaths, eliminate any mouth noise that I hear such as lip smacks and clicks, and add some light compression to the entire finished file before saving it. Other talent may have different ideas about this process. My own goal is to give an editor a high quality recording of useable reads to work with. This will save him from having to spend time trying to correct any problems with the recording and still allow him to "sweeten" the tracks as he sees fit; that is, make any desired adjustments to the sound using equalization, compression, filtering, etc.

Remember, the amount of time you have to turn around an audition once you've received that e-mail request is pretty short; within the hour at most and usually quicker than that. Sooner is always going to be better if you want to be the early bird that gets the worm.

It Takes Time To Become An Overnight Sensation

Even if you do a lot of scratching on a particular film, your reads are great, and the editor at the production house thinks you sound terrific too, the studio may choose someone else to provide the final voice for a project even if that person didn't do any early scratch work on it. It can take a long time for the industry to give a new talent a real, live job. This can be frustrating. As I said at the beginning of the book, it's very competitive at the top of the Voice Over Pyramid. This is why persistence over the long term, a healthy dose of self esteem, and belief in your own talent are essential. The studio's paying the bills, and they get the final say in the matter.

I do a lot of scratching for horror and suspense films. My voice is naturally gravelly and gritty and has become more so with age. Several years ago, I was at a party where I happened to meet one of the guys who finishes (gets the final booking) on the TV spots for a lot of the darker, scarier movies. I'd always heard he was a great guy and had wanted to meet him.

We struck up a conversation about a bunch of stuff including the fact that he'd once worked as an editor for a TV station in my hometown of Boston. He knew how editors think and what they're looking for in a read.

"Ya know," I said, "I scratch on a lot of the movies you end up finishing on."

"Really?," he replied. "That's gotta piss you off!" We both chuckled, raised our glasses and kept on talking.

Was I really pissed off? Well, not really. I wasn't angry at the guy for booking all the work I was scratching on. I was glad he did so well. He's one of my voiceover heroes, and I told him that. Frustrated sometimes? Disappointed? Sure. That's only natural.

You will probably do a lot of scratching before you book you first paid job. Winning the actual job is like winning the lottery. But the great benefit of scratching regularly is that you get *heard* by the folks at the trailer production houses and (if you're lucky) by the heads of marketing at the studios themselves. They are the ultimate decision makers who will book you for a film's campaign. All it takes is one studio executive who wants to take a chance on a newer voice.

CHAPTER 6

You Booked It!

*"Alright, Mr. DeMille,
I'm ready for my closeup."*

(SUNSET BOULEVARD, 1950)

So you finally get the call from your manager, "You're being considered for a campaign!"

Unless you're one of the well known heavy hitters who are simply handed a campaign, this is probably a film you've scratched on. The production house has developed a short list of contenders (or maybe only a list of one) that it wants to appear in their final edits being presented to the studio. The marketing executives will make the final selection for the voice of the film's campaign. All the training, patience, and hard work has paid off. Yay for you!

As they saying goes, "It's an honor just to be nominated," but naturally you'd really love the actual gig! My advice is to hold your horses and keep your expectations in check. Another voice might be in consideration too, including one of the "whales," the pros who have been voicing trailers for a long time.

You just never really know what's going on behind the scenes. As someone newer to the game, what you really want is to be an option for a studio marketing executive. If they're thinking of trying something different and are willing to give a new voice a chance, you want to be a possible choice. You want to make their decision to hire you look and feel like a stroke of genius.

With all of the other work you're doing on a daily basis (auditions, scratches for other films, marketing, commercial sessions) you might have even forgotten that you'd read any scripts for this project at all. You may have gone for many weeks or even months without hearing a word.

Now you wait for one of three things to happen:

- You hear nothing more and eventually hear another voice on the campaign.
- Your manager receives a courtesy call that the studio has "gone in another direction" and chosen a different voice.
- YOU GET THE JOB!

Let's go with option number three. Chances are you're going to be voicing the TV, digital and radio spots for the campaign in addition to any online and in-theater assets. The first thing you need to do, especially if this is a film you're not familiar with, is to find out all you can about it!

As we learned earlier, you should be able to find at least one trailer already online that was published long before the studio needed to make a decision on who would voice any of the other marketing elements. This will be valuable to see.

Check out IMDb for information on the film. What's the plot? Are there any major stars attached to it? Is it a high profile director? Again, all of this information will give you an idea of the kind of copy that will soon be coming your way.

Your Pay And The Responsibilities That Come With It

You're going to be paid well. Whether you'll be paid on a per spot basis or your manager has negotiated a package deal that calls for a certain number of spots, you're going to discover one of the reasons people want to try and break into the tip of the Voice Over Pyramid.

My fee is usually well above union scale for each spot I finish on, and I'm happy to get it! I've also worked on some campaigns with package deals worth many tens of thousands of dollars. Be grateful. Not everyone gets to earn a living the way we do.

You're being paid, in part, to be available twenty-four hours a day. A campaign starts with a pre-planned number of trailers or TV spots, but more may be added. There also might be changes to copy you've already recorded. These are needed yesterday. Be prepared to leave a restaurant on a Saturday evening when you get a call or e-mail asking you to voice a new line or even just a couple of words. Being available and reliable makes everyone else's jobs that much easier and makes you look really, really professional. Don't be the one who makes it difficult to get the work done. And *never* go on vacation while you're on a campaign!

Most of the time you'll be recording on your own from your home studio. Sometimes you'll be requested for a live session with the production house or studio via ISDN or an equivalent. In those sessions you'll be directed and they will record the tracks at their end. This happened when I was working on the "A House With a Clock In Its Walls" campaign. I recorded the initial work and it was used in the spot that got me on the campaign. When Universal decided to create more spots with the style of read I'd given them, I did many sessions reading different copy via ISDN to their recording studio on the lot so they could produce the spots they wanted.

If you're recording yourself, remember to always save your work as a .wav file, not an .mp3. This is an uncompressed file format and is much higher quality. This higher quality will allow the editor or audio engineer to more easily manipulate the tracks as needed. Because you're not reading to footage of the actual trailer or TV spot (known as reading to picture), many times your delivery needs to be sped up in order to fit within the structure of the final edit. A .wav file allows for that without any loss in quality.

Be a good friend to your editor. They need options, lots of them. Just like we talked about in the chapter on scratching, record a few takes of the spot at regular speed, then record a few more quickly. Do three in a row of each line in which you vary the way you say them, even slightly. Are the film's stars mentioned? Record their names a few times with different inflections. If you're recording a line with a pause, go ahead and give another take without the pause or vice versa. A good editor will pull together the parts he needs to create just the right read for the spot.

Once the campaign is finished and the movie has opened, thank people! Your manager can help coordinate this. Gift cards, gift baskets, tickets to a show or a ballgame, anything you can do to show your appreciation and gratitude to the people who trusted you will go a long way toward creating goodwill. You'll need them to think of you for your next job. I always send a handwritten thank you note to the studio marketing team. It only takes a minute, and only costs a stamp.

CHAPTER 7

Sustaining A Career

"May The Force be with you."

(STAR WARS, 1977)

According to the dictionary, a career is defined as "an occupation undertaken for a significant period of a person's life and with opportunities for progress."

The key word for me there is *opportunities*. How do you take advantage of the opportunities that come your way, and use them to help your career grow? Having a career as a voice actor means your progress can be measured in a number of ways. No two careers are identical, so progress can look different from one career to another.

The route to success, whatever you define that to be, can be challenging and circuitous, but if the trend over the long term is up, that's a good thing. You need to practice the fine art of perseverance while facing rejection and forces completely out of your control. It's not always easy.

In the world of trailers, the tip of the Voice Over Pyramid, you can't do it alone. You need your team in place to help you find the opportunities that are right for you and leverage them as best you can.

Here are some things that I've kept in mind. They help me to stay positive, and I think they'll help you too.

Don't Compare Yourself to Others

No two careers are alike and comparing your career journey to someone else's will only cause of frustration. This business is full of imponderables, and there can be exceptions to just about everything I've talked about in this book. As in life, some are in front of you and others are behind you. There is no one perfect formula for getting ahead.

Watch And Learn

This is your homework. You can find so many trailers, old and recent, online. Take a little time each day to check them out. Listen for trends. Are certain voices used for certain types of films? Are certain read styles more appropriate for certain film genres? Learn to fine tune your trailer read by immersing yourself in actual trailers.

Practice at Home

Go an extra step and transcribe some of the trailers you watch so you can practice in your home studio. Start by imitating trailers you've heard. Practice your Pauses, Leans, Rules of Three, and Eyebrow Raises. Now listen back. With time and increased confidence, you'll be able to make the copy your own without simply mimicking what you heard someone else do.

Take A Class or Seminar

The great benefit of a class or group workshop is that you get to learn from others, and they get to learn from you. You get both subjective learning (you working in the booth with the director) and objective learning (you watching other people work in the booth). I guarantee you'll learn more from watching others from outside the booth than you will standing in front of the microphone yourself. It sounds counterintuitive, but it's true.

Work With a Coach

Private coaching is great when you have a particular issue you want to work on. A good coach will be the objective ear that can help keep your reads fresh and keep you on top of current trends. Sometimes just a simple adjustment to your delivery can make all the difference.

But Don't Get Addicted to Coaching

This can be a danger, especially for beginners. Like therapy, coaching should help you identify and overcome issues with your delivery. But if you work with a coach constantly and never hear any progress, how are you benefiting? You may do great in a coaching session but if that work doesn't carry over to when you're recording in your own booth or at a recording session at a studio there's a problem.

Coaches obviously have a financial interest in having you as a client, but you can't pay them to be there for you on every audition or job. Eventually you need to have the skill and confidence to do the work on your own without a coach holding your hand. Reputable coaches will help you resolve your problem and invite you back for a checkup every now and then.

Participate in Your Own Career

You can't just sit around waiting for the phone to ring. You're in charge of your career so act like it. Check in with your reps from time to time without being a pest. Ask them if there's anything you can do to help them do their jobs. Work on your marketing. Freshen up your demo. Do some research into upcoming films you think would be a good fit for your voice. We can all do a little more. If you want to *be* busy, *get* busy.

Female Narrators

Now more than ever, women are finding seats on the trailer narrator bench. It is certainly still a male dominated profession and the reasons why are complex. But if you're a female talent who's curious about the trailer world, there's an admittedly tiny but expanding space at the tip of the Voice Over Pyramid just for you.

Trailers for Video Games

The gaming industry is enormous! I read recently that the profits from the sale of video games exceed those of the music and film industries *combined*. There are similarities in how films and games are marketed, particularly with the use of online trailers. You'll see a lot of those for new releases in larger game franchises that have huge, established fan bases.

Have an Attitude of Gratitude

Yes, it's a cliché, but if you're sincere about it, it shows others that you care about more than just yourself. Only you can decide how you show up in the world. How do you want to be perceived?

CHAPTER 8

The Future

"We know what we are but know not what we may be."

—**WILLIAM SHAKESPEARE**

Throughout this book, I've tried to give you a sense of what it takes to be a narrator for movie trailers and TV spots that market films. If you're currently a voice actor working in other areas of the business, you now have some solid foundational skills that will help you manage the path up to the tip of the Voice Over Pyramid. I've given you some history and an understanding of the way the industry works today, together with some practical tips on how to execute copy.

What will the trailer business look like decades from now? How about in just a few years? It's hard to know but as we've seen, things have changed a lot since the very first movie trailer was produced in 1913. The world has changed, technology has advanced, and my guess is that the way we all enjoy entertainment will change as time rolls on.

The advent of radio in the early days of the 20th century changed the way people consumed their entertainment. Then came television, first in black and white and then in full color, which changed things again. The digital age has brought us electronic devices with smaller screens and wireless

The Future

mobility that allow us to watch *what* we want *when* we want from just about anywhere.

What will be next? Holograms? Virtual reality trailer-like experiences that are customized just for us? Whatever there is, there will always be stories to tell and tickets to sell.

And voices will always be part of the package.

That's a wrap. Roll the credits.

www.ingramcontent.com/pod-product-compliance
Lightning Source LLC
LaVergne TN
LVHW051526070426
835507LV00023B/3328